THE PIT

PUBS

'The world affords not such inns
as England hath'

FYNES MORYSON – ELIZABETHAN ADVENTURER

The public house stands at the heart of
England's national life. It is an essential part
of the English scene and something that
people from all over the world come to
Britain to experience. The pub phenomenon
is a rich tapestry of many threads, the
complex tastes and aspirations of today's
changing times interwoven with the
innumerable deeds of our long and
chequered history. True, most countries have
places where you can buy a drink and enjoy
the company of friends. In some countries
people have even dared to imitate the pub.
But the real thing is unique and very special.
This book is an attempt to explain why.

What is a Pub?

• • • • • • • • • • • • • • • • • •

With a delightful irony, the one thing that makes the public house unique is that no two are ever the same. Indeed, most English pubs are as different one from another as beer is from bubblegum. Yet despite the rich array of hostelries, there are features common to them all that we can observe and rejoice in.

The first and crucial thing is that a public house is just what it says, someone's house that is open to the public. A pub is not usually unlocked in the morning and abandoned, empty, at night. Almost always the owner or manager lives on the premises and, because it is someone's home, the true English pub acquires more of the character of the people that live and work there.

Like the biblical mansion, a public house has many rooms. Since Victorian times, most pubs have had several separate drinking areas taking up most of the ground floor. Many have further rooms upstairs or even in the basement. Inevitably, there are exceptions. In past times, many rural taverns had just one, maybe two small rooms – indeed a few precious examples still hide in country lanes for the fortunate traveller to discover. It is also true that some refurbished pubs have had all their smaller bars knocked through into one huge carpeted space. But more often than not, a pub has several areas to drink in, each with its own clientele and character.

Another identifying feature is that pubs were founded to sell beer. Happily, England is a land flowing with good ale, the character of which varies as much as the places that sell it – but more

The lonely Tan Hill Inn, at Keld near Reeth in the Yorkshire Dales, is Britain's highest inn, 528 metres (1,732 feet) above sea level. It provides a very welcome respite for walkers on the Pennine Way.

LEFT: The Baker's Arms at Broad Campden, Gloucester-shire, a fine Cotswold Inn.

RIGHT: The simple country alehouse is an almost extinct species. Until recently The Drewe Arms at Drewsteignton in Devon was a surviving example. The death of the nonagenarian landlady, 'Auntie' Mabel Mudge, has inevitably meant changes, but much charm remains.

about this wonderful drink later on. In recent years, other drinks have increased in popularity: spirits, wines, cider, cocktails – even alcoholic lemonade! – but suffice it for now to say that every true pub serves beer.

A vital part of the public house, perhaps the most important of all, is the person who runs it. However splendid the building or its furnishings, the landlord (or landlady!) can make or mar any pub. Despite the desire of some pub chains to spawn clone pubs of alien formula in every high street, the individuality of landlords still shines through.

ABOVE: The warmth of an English pub on a cold night offers an irresistible invitation to the thirsty passer-by.

RIGHT: The Red Lion at Snargate, standing on the edge of Romney Marsh in Kent, is 450 years old and has remained virtually unaltered since before the First World War.

Ale, Angles and Aristocrats

B eer was first brewed and enjoyed thousands of years ago. With the drink's spreading popularity, special places to consume it opened and prospered. There were beer houses in Babylon in 2000 BC and probably in Egypt even before that.

Despite their preference for wine, it was the Romans with the *taberna* (hence our word 'tavern') who did most to advance the cause of the pub in Britain. The legions that Claudius sent to invade in AD 43 brought with them many Roman ideas. The *taberna* was one, and it is thought that wine shops were set up at regular intervals along the military roads of Britain.

BELOW: Pubs often began as lodgings for church builders. This is likely in the case of the Drewe Arms, which got its heraldic title only in the 20th century, when Britain's last castle was built nearby.

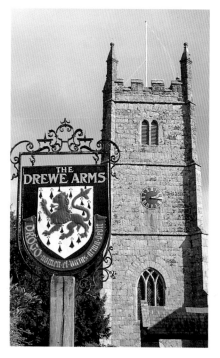

RIGHT: The Lamb and Flag emblem, from a pub in Cambridgeshire, indicates the hostelry's ecclesiastical origins.

By the 5th century the Romans had gone and for the next 500 years waves of Angles, Saxons and Danes came to terrorize, subdue and finally settle. Unlike their Mediterranean predecessors, these men were dedicated beer drinkers. Saxon women learned to brew just as they learned to bake – the word 'ale' comes from the Saxon *ealu* and the Danish *ol.*

Inevitably, some lady 'brewsters' were better than others and it was in their homes that people gathered to swap stories and drink beer. It is from this thousand-year tradition that the unique concept of public houses – houses open to the public – developed.

Unlikely as it may seem, the Church played an important part in the history of the pub. Throughout medieval England, churches and monasteries grew and flourished. Visitors, whether traders, pilgrims or official guests, needed food, drink and a place to sleep. Church stonemasons and carpenters could not work on empty stomachs. So public houses were established by abbeys and cathedrals, many of them run by ecclesiastical hosts and given names with religious themes.

A third important strand of pub history was the growth of large estates owned by the landed gentry. Estate workers, like many of their lay counterparts in religious establishments, received part of their wages and rations in the form of beer. This was brewed and drunk at a public house on or close by the estate, owned by and named after the lord of the manor.

RIGHT: Ye Olde Trip to Jerusalem, Nottingham, is perhaps the leading contender for the title of oldest pub in England. Its rooms extend into ancient caves beneath the hillside.

LEFT: The George Inn at Norton St Philip, Somerset, was built in 1397 by Carthusian monks as a guest house for visiting wool merchants. The Duke of Monmouth stayed here before the Battle of Sedgemoor of 1685.

ABOVE: Hunting has traditional connections with the local tavern.

Ale and Beer

At first, ale and beer were two different things. Until the Middle Ages, English ale was brewed without hops. The original drink, brewed with hops as a flavouring and preservative, was imported from the Low Countries in the 15th century. Over a period of 150 years, hops came to be accepted as a vital part of the drink; ale and beer became synonymous.

The Travellers' Rest

In medieval times people travelled for business, not pleasure. Early inns reflected this in their spartan simplicity. Beds would be straw pallets on a stone floor strewn with rushes. Several people slept in one room, men and women alike. Each guest brought or purchased his own food, which was cooked individually to order, and eaten alone.

As travelling increased in the 15th and 16th centuries, so did the number and quality of roadside inns. Carpets and decorations made their appearance. Food took on a new importance, and many a landlord's table groaned with produce from the locality – goose, swan, lark, lamprey, sturgeon, olive pie, nectarines, saffron cake –

A mail coach prepares to set forth from Ye Olde Cock Tavern in Fleet Street, London. The tavern moved over the road in 1887, but retains its character even today.

the list goes on. Today, eating an eight-course meal might seem like gluttony, but then it was not. Huge repasts were a way of passing time which may otherwise have hung heavily. Strolling players and musicians would often entertain the diners between and during courses.

Yet it was comfort rather than cuisine that was an inn's biggest selling point, and the notice 'Good beds' was a common sight along British highways.

The 1663 Turnpike Act improved roads, making coach travel quicker and smoother. A century later, mail coaches were introduced. The journey from London to Bristol took less than 24 hours. Every 15 miles (24 km) or so, the horses were changed, which was how the coaching inn came into existence.

The blare of a post-horn in the distance would announce an impending arrival, and shortly the coach and four would sweep triumphantly into the inn yard.

In those days, 'mine host' was truly that. Traditionally, the innkeeper would

ABOVE: The Garrick Inn at Stratford-upon-Avon. Many of Shakespeare's plays were performed in the galleried yards of coaching inns.

meet his guests personally as they alighted from the coach. The inn yard came instantly alive as a bustling army of waiters, grooms, chambermaids, cooks and postillions appeared to attend to the new arrivals. Hot meals awaited the hungry traveller at any time, day or night. But this clamour and bustle was destined to die away, and soon.

In the 1820s the alien sounds of a steam train first startled the countryside. Within 30 years rail travel, faster and more comfortable than coach and horses, had seen off its old-fashioned rival. As railwaymania gathered momentum, fine coaching inns perished. Great was the mourning at their demise. As one Victorian observer put it, 'The old idea of the inn was sacrificed to the genius of locomotion'.

ABOVE: As rail travel became popular, the coach trade disappeared and many hitherto prosperous wayside inns were left to the locals.

Come here, my sweet landlady, pray how d'ye do?
Where is Cicely so cleanly, and Prudence and Sue?
And where is the widow that dwelt here below?
And the ostler that sung about eight years ago?

Why now let me die, Sir, or live upon trust,
If I know which question to answer you first;
Why things since I saw you, most strangely have varied,
The ostler is hanged and the widow is married;
And Prue left a child for the parish to nurse,
And Cicely went off with a gentleman's purse.

MATTHEW PRIOR

Signs of the Times

Pubs can always be distinguished from other buildings by the sign hanging outside. The origin of pub signs goes back to the very origins of pubs themselves.

The Romans, when new wine had been delivered, used to hang a bundle of vine leaves on a chain outside the *taberna*. In Saxon England lady brewsters identified their houses with an ale stake, a wooden pole sticking out of the roof or standing upright in the ground. In the Roman tradition, there would be leaves, vines or maybe a decorative garland at the end of the pole.

The practice became a matter of law in 1393 when Richard II decreed that all taverns should display a sign, either suspended from a protruding beam or perched on a free-standing pole outside. This was so that ale-conners (the official samplers of beer) should know where to go to do their testing. Also, if the establishment lost its licence, all would know as the sign could be removed.

In those days few people could read, so the symbols chosen were simple and familiar, naturally tending to reflect the origins and ownership of the establishment concerned. Often signs were objects rather than painted representations. Those for hostelries set up by churches and abbeys almost always had

ABOVE: In Saxon times an alehouse was identified by its ale stake, a wooden pole with leaves or vines at the end.

ABOVE: The popular pub name The Bush derives directly from the vegetation at the end of the Saxon ale stake.

a religious tone – the Crossed Keys (to the kingdom of heaven), the Lamb, or the Bull (a *bulla* was an ecclesiastical seal). Inns set up by large estates tended to adopt more earthly symbols for their identity – the Plough, the Crook & Shears, the Cow – or even just a twisted piece of wood (the pub name 'The Crooked Billet' means just that). It was just as likely that they would display the coat of arms of the lord of the manor, hence names like the Oxenham Arms, the Wilton Arms and so on.

In the 17th century, competition between pubs, and particularly between coaching inns, became fiercer

We are not amused

Queen Elizabeth I, as she travelled the highways of her realm, was dismayed by the way she was depicted on inn signs. She therefore issued one approved likeness which everyone had to copy. Her descendant, Queen Victoria, was not amused by seeing herself and her relatives on pub signs, and banned the practice of depicting living royalty. The rule still applies.

RIGHT: Pubs were often places where men belonging to a particular trade gathered: to be hired, to be paid, to air their common grievances. Where this happened, the pub would often assume a bogus heraldic identity related to the trade concerned.

than ever. Inn signs reflected the determination to catch trade, being extremely ornate affairs overhanging the street. One such sign in Fleet Street collapsed, taking the front wall of the inn with it and killing two women, a cobbler and the king's jeweller. Because of the dangers involved, a Parliamentary Act of 1667 forbade any further building of these 'gallows' signs and restricted the size to the modest 4 feet by 3 feet (1.2m x 1m) now familiar today. Today's signs provide a colourful addition to the English scene and a lively reflection of our chequered past.

RIGHT and BELOW:
A pub's name can be inter-
preted in different ways. No
doubt both 'Wellingtons'
were named after the
English hero, but one sign
has received a 20th-
century twist.

WELLINGTON INN

It was quite usual for the signs of coaching inns to straddle the highway, for it was important to catch the attention of the driver of a coach and four in full flight sufficiently soon for him to bring his team to a halt. The sign here, the most elaborate ever devised, was erected in 1655 by John Peck of The White Hart (now the Scole Inn) at Scole in Norfolk. Besides the hart itself, within an ale garland, various stories from Greek mythology are depicted – Charon and Cerberus, Diana and others. The sign cost over £1,000, or £100,000 by today's standards.

BELOW: Another clever twist to a simple name. A beer engine is the hand pump used to draw beer, but the railside location of this pub near Exeter led to a different interpretation on the sign.

THE BEER ENGINE

A Rich History of Names

For many centuries the name of a pub counted for little. As few people could read, the communicative power of the sign outside was the important factor. But wider literacy in the 19th century opened the door to all sorts of new and imaginative names; these days there are thousands of them.

Names with heraldic connections are common, often the symbols of former heroes. For example, the Sun was the badge of Richard the Lionheart, the Feathers that of the Black Prince. The White Horse originally adorned Saxon banners, while the Rose was the emblem of the Tudors.

Royalty in general is a rich source. The Red Lion, the most popular name of all, was the badge of John of Gaunt and later of King James I. The Royal Oak, almost as common, reminds us how the future Charles II hid from Cromwell's men in a Shropshire oak tree during the Civil War.

Occupations gave many pubs their names – The Saddler's Arms, The Jolly Hatters, The Woodman and so on. This comes from the time when tradesmen would gather in one particular pub where wages would be paid, men hired and grievances discussed. The name of the trade and that of the pub would become inextricably linked.

Many pubs pay tribute to historic events and people, with names like Ye Olde Trip to Jerusalem (i.e. the Crusades), The Admiral Nelson and The Mafeking Hero. However The George and Dragon, The Robin Hood and The King Arthur show that existence in legend only is quite enough to qualify for licensed immortality. Historical changes would often result in sudden renamings. The many Pope's Heads soon became King's Heads when Henry VIII severed his connections with Rome. Unsurprisingly, inns named The Crown soon disappeared after the execution of King Charles I!

ABOVE: Pub names often echo historical links. This Winchester pub commemorates King Henry III, who was born in the city and often stayed in the castle there.

There are many other themes for pub names, including field sports (e.g. Dog & Duck, Fox & Hounds); nautical (e.g. Hope & Anchor, Compass); food and drink (e.g. Haunch of Venison, Cheshire Cheese); show-business (e.g. Charlie Chaplin's, Sir Alfred Hitchcock); transport (e.g. Atmospheric Railway, Shroppie Fly) or the world of literature (e.g. David Copperfield, Good Companions). The Sherlock Holmes in Northumberland Street, Central London includes a museum and a re-creation of the famous detective's sitting room and study.

RIGHT: As The Northumberland Arms, this London pub was mentioned in the Sherlock Holmes adventure, The Hound of the Baskervilles. Since 1957, it has commemorated the detective.

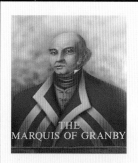

The Marquis of Granby

This 18th-century nobleman is now remembered only through the many pubs which were named after him as a mark of gratitude. Commander-in-Chief of the Army in 1766, Granby set up many of his soldiers as tavern keepers when they retired from service.

THE MARQUIS OF GRANBY

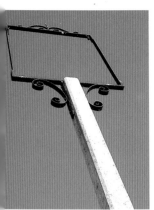

LEFT: *The absent sign is not an indication of yet another pub closure. Rather it announces 'the pub with no name', officially The White Horse at Priors Dean, Hampshire. The sign came down many years ago and was never replaced!*

During the Napoleonic War a prison camp for French officers was set up at Biddenden in Kent. Prisoners were on trust to walk only as far as an alehouse at a three-way junction, known to them as *les trois chemins*. Locals pronounced this in the only way they could handle!

In recent years, pub names have become more adventurous – try The Jet and Whittle (Leamington Spa), The Goldfinger Tavern (Highworth, Wilts) and The Twenty Churchwardens (Cockley Cley, Norfolk). Some of the latest ones are self-consciously offbeat, such as The Fuzz and Firkin (and many other 'Firkin' names), Brain Surgery near Bath or The Bull and Spectacles (Blithbury, Staffs).

Before the First World War, The Belgian Arms at Holyport, Berkshire was known as The Eagle. German prisoners-of-war, out exercising from a nearby camp, used to annoy the locals by saluting the eagle on the inn sign (the Eagle was also the Prussian emblem). So the pub's name was hastily changed to honour Belgium, at the time resisting a German invasion.

BELOW: *Although the sign, at one time hung upside down, makes play of the 'mad' meaning of 'barmy', the name comes from 'barm', the froth on fermenting beer.*

A Tavern in the Town

● ● ● ● ● ● ● ● ● ● ● ● ● ● ● ● ● ●

RIGHT: The immaculate mahogany of one of London's many beautifully preserved City taverns. These places lead double lives — lunchtime talking shops for business people and evening haunts for pleasure seekers.

These days, many public houses are not what they seem. Seeking a night's rest, you may walk into what calls itself an inn or a hotel, only to find yourself in a simple alehouse with no beds to be had. Blame history for this.

In the past, names like tavern, inn and hotel distinguished hostelries with different licences. An inn was a place bound by law to feed and welcome wayfarers by day or by night. The tavern, on the other hand, was a place of casual refreshment, a jolly rendezvous where townsmen could enjoy food, drink and good company, but only during set hours.

With the passage of time, the inn has kept its place in society. Surviving old inns of England are the subject of much veneration, photographed and written about in coffee-table books throughout the land. The tavern, on the other hand, has fallen from grace. London alehouses used to be the meeting-places of the mighty; Shakespeare and Sheridan, Raleigh and Reynolds, Garrick and Goldsmith all had their favoured taverns. Over a pint of ale, mulled wine, egg-hot or suchlike, the great and good gathered to debate the issues of the day. Government policy was often made in taverns; plays and periodicals were often written over tankards of ale.

ABOVE: Before the days of the gentleman's club, London's taverns were the haunts of the great and good.

BELOW: In the 1820s the tavern was not the fashionable place it had once been.

Straight or Handle?

There are two common types of drinking vessels for beer, one with straight sides (usually called a glass) and one with a handle (usually known as a mug or a pot). When asked the question 'Straight or handle?', many drinkers have no preference – just so long as the beer is wet and tastes like beer! Others have very decided views. 'Straight' devotees feel beer tastes better from a thinner glass; 'handle' people maintain that grasping a straight glass alters the beer's temperature.

Late in the 17th century, things began to change. Tea and coffee houses opened in the City (the now famous Lloyd's being one of them). Merchants and burgesses began to desert their previous haunts for these new, fashionable venues. In the 18th century, gentlemen's clubs began to appear: Crockford's, the Athenaeum, the Garrick, each creating its own milieu. Seduced by this hushed new world of carpets, leather and servile discretion, men of wealth and creativity turned their backs on mere drinking houses. Those who 50 years earlier would have been certain tavern men now became club men.

For taverns, there was only one way to go, and that was down. They came to be thought of as 'low'. The institution which had previously been at the forefront of fashion became, by mid-Victorian times, the humble pub.

RIGHT: Some breweries still make town deliveries in the traditional way. Here, Vaux dray horses plod through the streets of Sunderland.

The Rise of the Gin Palace

The accession of William and Mary in 1689 dealt a double blow to lovers of English ale. To finance the king's infamous Irish campaigns, heavy duties were imposed on beer. Worse still, the royal couple from Holland had made fashionable the Dutch drink of gin. In 1690 Parliament gave all citizens the right to distil liquor, so long as they used English corn. Pandora's Box was opened.

London was soon awash with untaxed gin as over 9,000 dram-shops sprang up in the capital. *Gin Lane*, Hogarth's famous drawing of alcoholic ruin, graphically illustrated the problems. Beer, by curious contrast, came to be thought of as relatively respectable.

By 1830, the situation was somewhat better, but the new Prime Minister, the Duke of Wellington, sought a final cure. A Parliamentary Act of that year freed beer from both licensing laws and duty. The results were catastrophic. Within a year, 30,000 new beer-shops had opened throughout England. Retaliation from the dram-shops followed. They went up-market, introducing expensive features such as carpets, mirrors, engraved glass and brass fittings and soon acquiring the sobriquet 'gin palaces'.

At a similar time, another important and lasting change was taking place. Originally, beer had been brewed individually on the premises of each pub. But now, brewing had become big business, too big for pubs to handle on their own. All over Britain, specialist brewers set themselves up to cope with growing demand, and families such as Bass, Whitbread, Charrington and Watney were already becoming household names.

In a world where drinking habits were changing rapidly, these brewers sought to stabilize their market position by buying up outlets for their beers, or at least by striking deals with public houses to sell only their products.

The acute competition from the gin palaces hastened this process. To survive, publicans needed to renovate their premises, but few had the resources to do it. Selling out to a brewery or striking a deal as a 'tied house' was often the only way to keep the bailiff from the door.

RIGHT: In the early 18th century, taverns had a far more orderly image and reputation than that of the gin palaces.

Tokens

In 1648 a shortage of small coins and precious metals led to individual pubs and other trades issuing tokens. These bore the value – a farthing, a halfpenny or a penny – on one side and, on the reverse, the name of the tavern. They remained in legal use until 1674 and often became currency in the area around the establishment concerned.

LEFT: William Hogarth's classic drawing of 1751, Gin Lane, illustrating in his inimitable way the appalling social problems caused by the unlimited availability of untaxed gin. The Dutch drink came into fashion after 1689, the time of William and Mary's joint reign. Soon 9,000 dram-shops had sprung up in London alone.

RIGHT: Taverns gained an ill reputation in Victorian times.

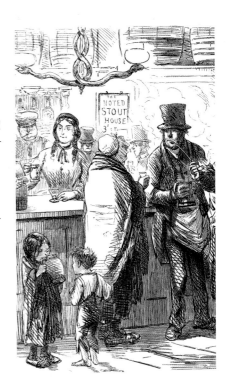

'Free House'

Many pub signs bear the phrase 'free house', but sadly, this does not mean that drinks within cost nothing! The term means less now than it once did. Most pubs are 'tied' to a brewer, whose name will often be displayed outside the pub. This means that the pub will sell one brewer's beer almost exclusively. Technically, a free house is one that is not tied to a particular brewer, and may therefore offer a wider range of beers. However, many belong to pub chains or have struck deals with brewers themselves, so the choice of beers may prove to be as limited as before.

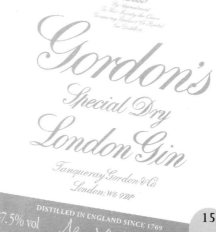

Pub Games

The English love games, and nowhere is this more evident than in the convivial atmosphere of the English pub. Some pub games are confined to certain regions – games with wonderful names like Knur and Spel and Devil among the Tailors. Yet there are many which can be found up and down the country.

The game of skittles is one of these. There are many varieties, but all involve propelling a solid missile, usually a ball, at upstanding targets. Skittle alleys of up to 14 metres (45 feet) in length can be found, especially in the West Country, where the game is most popular. Elsewhere miniature bar versions such as Devil among the Tailors exist, although these are becoming harder to find.

Much easier to find is the ancient game of Shove-Ha'penny. With the heel of the hand, players push smooth coins or discs across the polished surface of a 50–60 cm (18–24 inch) long board into zones of the 'beds', the scoring area. The winner is the first to 'shove' three coins into each zone.

ABOVE: The Bat and Ball, near Hambledon, Hampshire. The pub was the birthplace of organized cricket, which is still played on the green outside.

ABOVE: Beryl Cook's painting 'Bar Billiards' captures the atmosphere of pub games.

BELOW: Even the Vicar joined in this pre-war game of dominoes. The pegboard would also be used to score in cribbage.

Even the mildest pub games once faced opposition from Crown or clergy. From medieval to Jacobean times, almost all pub games were illegal. While Henry VIII and his ancestors enjoyed their games of real tennis and croquet, their subjects were forced to spend their spare time with a longbow, ready for the call to arms. In later times, pressure for legal restraints came from a puritanism which considered the whole concept of pubs and their games to be ungodly.

LEFT: A game of Shove Ha'penny. In this very old game, players propel a coin or disc with the heel of the hand to land precisely within certain zones of the board. Many pub games, such as the various types of bar skittles, are intriguing table-top miniatures of larger games.

BELOW: New pubs, old traditions. The latest generation of 'fun' pubs has brought a crop of new pub games.

Darts, like Shove-Ha'penny, is a pastime of great antiquity, and is still today the archetypal pub game. It is a rare pub that does not have a dart board in the corner and a set of 'arrows' available. Like skittles, it is often the subject of fiercely competitive league play. There are many different games and even several types of board.

Despite the pressures for change imposed on pubs in recent years, dominoes, like darts, has remained popular. Again, most pubs have a set of 'doms' (or 'tiles' or 'spots' or 'bones') behind the bar. The version often played in pubs is Fives and Threes, the object being to make the two ends of the domino chain add up to a multiple of either number.

Cards, of course, remain universally popular, the stakes being strictly limited by law. Cribbage, with its pegged wooden scoring board, is perhaps the most regularly played pub card game.

A pool table, too, is a common sight in the public bar these days, particularly attractive to younger customers. A puzzling and more traditional variant of this is bar billiards, identifiable by holes in the green baize table, guarded by mushroom-like pegs. Cueing from the same end at all times, players have to hit a ball down one of the holes without knocking over a peg.

RIGHT: Darts. One player throws from the line, or oche (say 'ocki'), while the other chalks up the score.

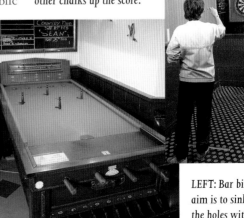

LEFT: Bar billiards. The aim is to sink the ball in the holes without hitting the pegs in front.

Urban Splendour

ABOVE: The Black Friar, situated near Blackfriars Bridge in London, has countless fine Art Nouveau features.

ABOVE: One of the many splendid pubs built on street corners in Victorian times to meet the rapid growth in population.

BELOW: The elegant glass, mirrors and brasswork of many 19th and early 20th-century town pubs were often destroyed as refurbishment took place in the post-war years. Thankfully, these features are now treasured.

After Prime Minister Wellington's liberating 1830 Act, the war of public house versus gin palace gathered momentum. Heavy investment of brewery money resulted in a proliferation of new or rebuilt pubs, many on the same proud lines as the new breed of dram-shops. In the provinces these appeared around market squares, on main highways, near docks and barracks and at the many newly fashionable seaside towns.

The Industrial Revolution was reaching its peak. Every week saw thousands of workers flooding into the cities from the countryside; they needed homes. To meet this demand, speculative builders threw up, with frightening haste, countless streets of terraced houses. At almost every street corner they built a pub. These 'locals' were an instant success, rapidly becoming the social hub of each newly created little community.

By the 1870s, the rise in living standards, particularly in industrial towns, meant that many of these locals became workers' palaces. Mahogany fittings, gleaming brasswork, engraved mirrors and windows, tiles and murals became the order of the day, all of it splendidly lit by gas.

HANDSOME TABLE,
MASSIVE
BRONZED STAND.
26-in. Circular Mahogany or Marble Tops, 22 6 each.
Similar, with 24-inch Tops, 21 - each.
22-inch Tops, 18/- each.

LEFT: An advertisement for the classic Britannia cast-iron pub table of the Victorian and Edwardian eras, still seen today. One recent trend in furnishing new pubs has been a simulated neglect, with no two chairs or tables being alike.

LEFT: No expense spared: the Victorian pub in all its splendour. Apart from the mosaic of the floor and bar, note the light fittings, the stained-glass coats of arms and the engraved window panels. This is The Philharmonic in Liverpool, a very famous city pub.

ABOVE: One of the titles given to the small private compartments in many Victorian pubs. But the privacy brought problems and in most pubs such rooms are a thing of the past.

BELOW: The magnificent floral display outside The Cask and Glass in Westminster.

The fashion was for pubs to have many small compartments, all served by a central serving 'island'. Some pubs had as many as 15 'boxes' – smoke rooms, parlours, tap rooms, snugs, news rooms and so on. In addition, most pubs of stature now included a large public room for meetings, music-hall, billiards and more. It was customary for public houses to play host to all manner of clubs and societies and, given the size and quality of the facilities, for all sorts of official business to be transacted on licensed premises. This included election meetings and inquests; even taxes were collected in pubs.

So the 'local' became the scene of all manner of official, commercial and social activity. Unfortunately, not all of it was respectable, a fact which was to cause disquiet in the Houses of Parliament.

From Blight to Block House

> 'We are fighting Germany, Austria and drink,
> and the greatest of these foes is drink.'
>
> DAVID LLOYD GEORGE, 1915

By 1900, pubs had hit an all-time low. Their small rooms were witness to all manner of theft, violence and sexual misbehaviour. Opening hours were long. Drunkenness was common.

In the First World War, drink was seen as such a threat to the war effort that in 1914 the Prime Minister, Lloyd George, severely curtailed opening hours (he even considered Prohibition). Only in recent years have these been relaxed.

But the war had liberating effects too. During the struggle, traditional restraints became irrelevant, and pubs came to be used by many whose parents would never have done so. After the war, thousands of 'Homes Fit For Heroes' were built; millions of people were on the move. These new flats and houses brought new pubs, larger, cleaner and brighter than anything seen before. Their architecture was elegant, their decor attractive. These were not dens of squalor and crime, but places where families could go in safety and comfort.

In the country things were changing too. Better bus and rail services in the 1920s took some pub customers away to the towns, but also brought people out of the towns to ramble. Charabancs took happy crowds on excursions. In the 1930s, the mass-produced cars of Messrs Ford and Morris made a day out in the country a weekly event for many families. All these people needed refreshment. The village pub was waking once more after a century of slumber.

Yet the professional classes still stayed away from pubs and many others preferred to entertain at home. The Second World War was to break this barrier for ever. Service men and women laughed, cried and drank together. For civilians, the Blitz brought not just bombs

The Carlisle Experiment

An historical quirk is that for most of the 20th century the government owned and ran pubs in Carlisle. During the First World War, the problem of drunkenness was particularly acute amongst munitions workers in the area. To exercise firmer control, the government bought up five breweries and 321 pubs there. Around 120 pubs were closed. Snugs, the small unsupervised rooms, were abolished. The remaining pubs were only sold back to brewers in recent years.

RIGHT: Not digging but knitting for victory! In both world wars the public house was a great source of cheer and comfort. But after the alcohol problems of the First War, the beer was at a reduced strength during the Second.

LEFT: The warm atmosphere of a pub in wartime.

RIGHT: Many roadhouses were built to cater for the pre-war boom in motoring.

BELOW: This depiction of a wartime icon illustrates effectively that pub signs are not great art, but in their caricatured naivety are an attractive artform in themselves.

Panel Licensing Laws

Licensing laws are by no means a recent invention. As early as the 10th century, the Saxon king Edgar decreed that ale-houses should be limited to one per village or small town. The Magna Carta of 1215 brought in a standard measure for ale and wine. Henry VIII declared that beer 'has always been a concern of the state' and rigorously controlled the quality and price of beer. By contrast, his daughter, 'Bloody' Mary I, tried unsuccessfully to restrict the number of pubs!

THE CHURCHILL ARMS

RIGHT: A popular poster image with its slogan embraces the spirit of wartime Britain.

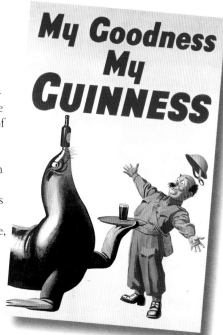

but boredom: long dark evenings at home, on watch or in the shelter. Non-essential travel was forbidden. In the 'blackout', cities were transformed into hundreds of discrete urban villages. At the heart of each was the local pub.

Bankers and butchers, colonels and coalmen all had to take their turn as fire-watchers, air raid wardens, Home Guard. After a spell on duty, it was only natural to relax together in the local. The pub was praised as being 'a block house on the home front', a far cry from its reputation just 25 years before.

It is easy to remember that the two World Wars destroyed people, homes and factories; it is easy to forget that they destroyed entrenched attitudes as well, and none more so than the popular attitude to drinking habits. During the war, the English pub acquired a respectability it has never lost.

'The one place where, after dark, the collective heart of the race could be seen and felt, beating resolute and strong.'

A.P. HERBERT, describing the English pub in the Second World War

21

The Strange World of the English Pub

Even in the eclectic world of the public house, some do stand out as being unusual. Here we present a selection.

The Red Lion at Avebury, Wiltshire is the only pub to be encompassed by a Neolithic stone circle, while down the road at Beckhampton is a Tudor inn, The Waggon & Horses, where Dickens stayed. He later wrote it into The Pickwick Papers. At Dorstone, near Hay-on-Wye, is The Pandy Inn, built by one of the knights that killed Archbishop Thomas Becket in 1170. The New Inn, in picturesque Clovelly, in Devon, is where Sir Walter Raleigh stayed on his honeymoon. At The Talbot, Oundle, Northamptonshire, one may tread the steps which Mary Queen of Scots descended to her execution in 1587.

A great number of pubs have bizarre histories and traditions of their own. Many were used for trials: The City Arms in Wells has a cell that was regularly used until 1810, and guilty men on the Isle of Wight were hanged at the Hare and Hounds in Newport. The lonely Warren House on Dartmoor has a fire which is never allowed to go out. The Olde Cross in Alnwick, Northumberland has had the same cobwebbed

RIGHT: The medieval Fleece Inn at Bretforton, Hereford & Worcester is owned by the National Trust, and is preserved much as it was in centuries gone by.

RIGHT: The Pilchard Inn on Burgh Island near Bigbury in Devon has to be reached by sea tractor when the tide is in.

bottles in the window for 200 years, as a fatal curse is said to fall on the person who moves them. The Busby Stoop, near Thirsk, North Yorkshire, is named after Tom Busby, who murdered his father-in-law and was hanged outside the pub in 1702. His stooping ghost still haunts the area with the hangman's noose round his neck! The Bull & Butcher at Turville, Buckinghamshire, is haunted by a former landlord, Lacey Beckett, who used to go riding dressed as Napoleon and in 1942 killed his wife, his dog and himself. Lacey's seat by the fire is still kept for him.

If you want a drink on a Sunday, stay away from The Chequers at Ledsham, West Yorkshire. In the 19th century a party of satisfied Sunday drinkers once went in for synchronized urination in the garden, in full view, it transpired, of the Lady of the Manor! In the village her word was law, and the pub has stayed shut on Sundays ever since.

RIGHT: The Castle Inn, between Stratford and Worcester, has obvious differences from the average pub!

Poetic Justice

The Swan at Grasmere was the scene of an embarrassing moment for the novelist Sir Walter Scott. His alcohol-free stay with the Wordsworths proved unbearable and he often surreptitiously nipped down to The Swan for a 'quick one'. Unfortunately he was with William Wordsworth when the poet went to hire a horse from the hostelry. The landlord said to a red-faced Scott that he was surprised to see him there earlier than usual!

LEFT: The Nutshell at Bury St Edmunds lays claim to being the smallest pub in England.

The Pub Today

· · · · · · · · · · ·

W hat of the English pub today? What changes, good or bad, have taken place over the last 50 years?

Sadly, in that period many public houses have closed their doors for ever. Particularly mourned is the passing of alehouses tucked away in tiny hamlets – no frills, no food, little profit, but good ales, good fellowship and the true scent of the countryside in every dusty corner. The few that even now survive are destined to die with their owners, or be changed beyond recognition.

The Beer Orders of 1990 were a response to the monopolistic nature of pubs being tied to a single brewery. Large brewers were forced to sell off many of their pubs. In theory, this created many more free houses, but these were often sold to newly created pub chains, not brewers themselves but almost as restrictive in their effect on the pubs they owned.

One result of this change is the corporate theme pub – American, Irish, Australian, whatever. A winning formula has tended to be repeated throughout the land. Books are bought by the yard, farm implements by the trailer load, boomerangs by the ton. To the purist, this may not be what the English pub is all about, but such places are very popular with many. Besides, there are many more traditional pubs

ABOVE: The prevalence in Britain of Australian lager, wines and TV soaps has encouraged some chains to create pubs with an antipodean atmosphere. Perhaps not for the purist, these have nevertheless proved very popular with the young generation.

RIGHT: The last years of the 20th century have seen many imaginative conversions of town centre buildings into lively young people's pubs. Decoration has tended to take one of two directions: for less architecturally remarkable places, a minimalist approach such as that pictured here; for grander premises a more sumptuous furnishing aimed at recapturing former days of splendour.

Mine Host

These days the person running a pub may be male or female, solo or in tandem; pub life is all the richer for that. The key factor is not gender or marital status, but personality. A successful 'mine host' must be welcoming yet not effusive, ready to talk or to listen, never be bored or boring. A good landlord should cherish the drink he purveys, having the skill and knowledge to select and serve it in a perfect state.

Wherever alcohol is consumed, restraint and discipline are needed. Although drink is his life and work, the landlord should never over-indulge himself. Customers must behave themselves too, and a good landlord sees that they do, in the gentlest possible way – the iron hand in the velvet glove. A successful publican has to be all things to all men.

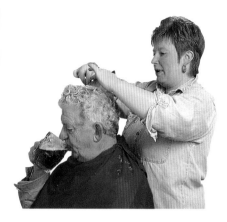

ABOVE: Pubs have traditionally filled many roles in the community. The closure of village shops and post offices in the face of competition from supermarkets has made the survival of the pub even more important.

for dissenters to drink at. In many towns and villages, institutions and businesses are under threat from superstores, hypermarkets and other ventures of profit-focused multinationals. In the face of this, pubs remain as a defiant beacon of local life, often having to act as post offices, banks, surgeries, youth clubs, sports clubs, and even churches!

Pub activities are legion: a tour of just one town's pubs might reveal anything from karaoke to cribbage, darts to discos, skittles to strippers!

BELOW: Irish theme pubs in many English towns and cities have brought a touch of Celtic magic into the lives of many young people.

A Cause for Celebration

• •

English beer is as good as it has ever been. In 1971, CAMRA, the Campaign for Real Ale, was founded to head off a move by the large national breweries towards selling only pressurized keg beer which had less taste but a longer shelf-life. The battle was won and today CAMRA is a reassuring watchdog against anything which threatens the traditional British pint. Largely thanks to their efforts, most pubs worth visiting now have at least two traditional cask-conditioned ales.

An apparently beneficial measure following from the Beer Orders was the insistence that pubs belonging to the largest brewers should be free to sell at least one 'guest beer', a cask-conditioned ale from a source other than the owning brewery. Despite the best efforts of some of the brewing giants to get round this by supplying their own 'guests', many excellent new independent breweries have opened in unlikely places, and some pubs have an impressive range of 'real' ales to choose from. Also the brew-pub has appeared once more. In 1841, 27,000 pubs still brewed their own beer. By the early 1970s only four worthy survivors remained. Now, thanks to the Beer Orders, the total is well over 100.

LEFT: Part of an old pictorial and poetic guide to English ale.

Cider, a traditional drink made from fermented apples, must also be mentioned. 'Real' cider, as sold in the West Country, is a fine tipple, but caution is needed, for most of the cider marketed in pubs today is a gassy imitation of the real thing.

X, put on a barrel, is intended to tell The strength of the beer, and its flavour as well.

RIGHT: In the 1960s, beer drawn from the cask by the traditional beer engine was under threat. Thanks to CAMRA, the wood and brass pumps with their colourful clips still grace most bars in the land.

LEFT: The use of handpumps almost always indicates that 'real ale' is being served.

RIGHT: One of many imaginative pub conversions to have been undertaken in recent years. The designers' notion is to retain as much of the original character of the building as possible. This was unmistakably once a cinema. Often the name of the pub reflects the former use of the building.

ABOVE: Tegestology (beer mat collecting) is a popular hobby. This mat comes from one of the 200 or so small independent breweries established over the last 20 years.

Real Ale – what is it?

Although most pubs serve a variety of drinks, the most popular tipple continues to be beer. Standard beer (bitter as opposed to stout, wheat beer, barley wine and so on) is treated in two different ways, resulting in two entirely different products, cask-conditioned real ale and brewery-conditioned keg beer. Both are brewed from water, barley, hops and yeast, but there the similarity ends.

Cask-conditioned beer is usually fermented in traditional open vessels and always comes to maturity in the cask; more hops are often added, together with finings (which clarify the beer). Because fermentation is still continuing, considerable skill must be shown over the next few days in handling, stillaging and pegging the casks, thus ensuring that the beer 'peaks' at the right time. It is served by hand pump or straight from the cask, ideally at about 13°C. As it stays at its best for only a few days, a quick turnover is needed.

Brewery-conditioned beer, on the other hand, is usually fermented in closed containers, stored in tanks, then filtered and pasteurised to kill off the yeast, giving it a longer 'shelf-life'. It is sent to the pub 'bright', i.e. ready for consumption, and needs no special handling. It is almost always served chilled and by means of gas pressure. All of this takes a severe toll on the flavour, but many still choose it.

To the connoisseur of English beer, the only worthwhile pint is one of cask-conditioned ale, with its fresh, mature flavour, although the foreign visitor may take a while to get used to this. Perseverance is inevitably rewarded!

Food to the Fore

'**P**ub grub' is big business now. Even as late as the 1960s, the hungry drinker was lucky to be offered more than a sandwich or a ploughman's (see panel). Now most pubs serve meals – they have to from economic necessity. Many serve excellent food, some of them on a scale similar to the coaching inns of yesteryear. Purists may long wistfully for the days of cheese and pickle, but there is no doubt that the revolution in pub dining is enjoyed by many people who prefer the idea of eating out informally.

The Ploughman's Lunch

The Ploughman's Lunch, based on the medieval farm labourer's midday snack of bread and cheese, is almost universally available in pubs that serve food. Today the basic ploughman's is likely to include some mixed pickle, a pickled onion and a garnish of salad. Other varieties contain more exotic cheeses or cold meats.

LEFT AND BELOW: Not too long ago, it was almost impossible for the hungry pub customer to get more than very basic fare. Now most pubs serve meals, many of them at a very high standard. Wine too is an accepted staple drink in almost all but the most traditional of pubs.

LEFT: *Although at the dawn of the 21st century England's hostelries have an infinite number of identities, the Ivy Inn at Heddington, Wiltshire, pictured here, still typifies most people's idea of the true English pub – thatched roof, oak beams, log fires and a warm welcome.*

SOME USEFUL BOOKS

The Good Beer Guide (CAMRA): a truly independent guide to tracking down the best beer.
The Good Pub Guide (Ebury Press): a generally reliable guide to pubs that are a pleasure to drink, eat or stay in.

Passport to the Pub (Brewers and licensed Retailers Association): a guide to pub etiquette.
Good Pub Food (CAMRA): a guide to the best food pubs.
Room at the Inn (CAMRA): a guide to pub accommodation.

Known Treasures and Hidden Gems (CAMRA): a guide to London pubs.
The English Pub: a History (Hale): a detailed history of the pub.

Acknowledgements

The publishers gratefully acknowledge the help of Jeff Evans in checking the proofs, and the following for use of photographs:
Arcaid/Richard Bryant: 23–23 below; Bass Taverns: 17 centre right, 24 above and below, 25 below, 28 centre; The Bat and Ball, Hambledon: 16 above left; Bridgeman Art Library: front cover (above right) and 6 (Beaton-Brown Fine Paintings, London); Cephas: 17 below right; Collections: front cover (below left), 2 above, 18 below right, 19 above left, 25 above left; Philip Craven: 7 above; Fotomas/Barnaby's: 14–15 below, 23 below right; Fuller, Smith & Turner: 12–13 above; Robert Harding Picture Library: inside front cover/title page, 19 above right; Hulton Getty: 16 below, 17 above, 20 above and below, 26–27 above; Guinness, Great Britain: 21 below right; Images: 10–11 below, 19 below right; Licensee & Morning Advertiser: 28 above; Mary Evans Picture Library: 5 top right, 9 below left, 12 above and below, 14–15 above, 15 above right, 18 above right, 26 left, back cover; John McIlwain: 4 below, 8 below, 9 above left and below right, 10 above and below, 11 above left and below right, 13 above right (both), 18 above left, 21 centre, 23 above, 26 below right; National Hop Association (Steven Morris): 5 below right; Andrew Perkins: front cover (above left), 3 above and below, 4 above, 4–5 above, 8 centre, 15 centre right, 17 below centre, 22 above (left and right), 23 centre, 25 above right, 28–29; Pitkin Unichrome: 16–17 below centre; The Three Chimneys: 11 above right; Topham: 7 centre; United Distillers: 15 below right; Vaux: 13 below; Weidenfeld & Nicholson (by Derry Brabbs): 2 below; J.D.Wetherspoon: 27 above right, 28 below; Derek White: 3 centre left; Ye Olde Trip to Jerusalem: 5 below left.
'Bar Billiards' (front cover (below right) and page 16 (top right)), original publication, copyright © Beryl Cook 1998. Reproduced by arrangement with the artist c/o Rogers, Coleridge & White Ltd, 20 Powis Mews, London W11 1JN.
The illustration at the top of page 8 is by Roger Hutchins.

Written and edited by John McIlwain.
Designed by John Buckley.
Picture research by Kate Duffy.

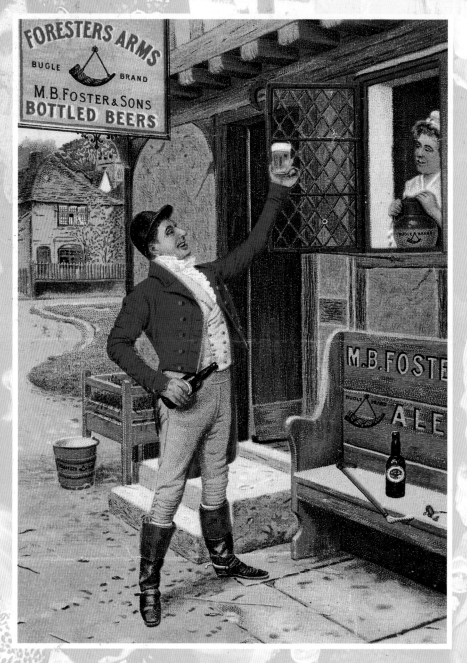

Public houses stand at the heart of English community life.
The thirsty traveller has rarely far to go before one appears
— a haven of warmth, welcome, rest and refreshment.
The English pub is a unique phenomenon, yet no two of them
are ever the same. This book traces their history — from ancient
Anglo-Saxon alehouses to the wild and wacky pubs of today.
Also within are some of the charming eccentricities which help
to keep the English pub so special and so dear to people's hearts.

PITKIN

ISBN 0-85372-882-8